MW00782235

PLANT-BASED DIET COOKBOOK RECIPES 2021

A Complete Cookbook with Easy and Mouth-Watering Plant-Based Meals

Alexia Wilson

Table of Contents

Introduction

Plant-based diets are becoming widely popular and more and more people are switching to plant-based diets for a variety of reasons. Diets that are based on consumption of plant foods and are rich in beans, nuts, seeds, fruit and vegetables, whole grains, and cereal based foods can provide all the nutrients needed for good health and offer affordable, tasty and nutritious alternatives to meat-based diets.

If you decided to switch to a plant-based diet you might be worried about amount of protein you consume. People who already follow vegan diet have learned how to get all needed nutrients from plant foods and supplements. But you are probably wondering: where to get protein from if you do not eat meat, fish, eggs and dairy products? Animal protein contains all the essential amino acids our body needs. However, these acids can be also obtained from plant foods. What's more, a plant-based diet can significantly diversify your diet in terms of protein sources.

List of Plant Based High Protein Products

There are a common misconception that vegetarian and vegan diets might be lacking sufficient amount of protein. However, many dietitians and scientists say that vegetarian or vegan diets have more than enough nutrients in them if planned well. Nevertheless, all foods are different in their protein values, there is food that contains more protein, and there are those that contain less.

Legumes or commonly known as beans have high amounts of protein per serving and contain 15 grams of protein per cooked cup. They are also a great source of iron, complex carbohydrates, folate, fiber, phosphorus, manganese and potassium. Can be used in a variety of recipes or eaten without anything else.

Nutritional yeast is another great source of protein. It has 14 grams of protein per 28 grams. It is also a great source of copper, magnesium, zinc, manganese and all B vitamins. It can be used in a variety of dishes and is sold as flakes and a yellow powder.

Next come lentils. They have 18 grams of protein per cooked cup. They also can be added to a whole variety of dishes. Lentils are also rich in iron, manganese and folate.

Tempeh, tofu, and edamame are another great source of protein. They are made from whole soybeans, which means they provide all the important amino acids. All three have 10-19 grams of protein per 100 grams, calcium and iron. Edamame needs to be steamed or boiled before eating and can be eaten without anything else or incorporated into soups and salads. Tofu and tempeh can also be used in lots of recipes.

Hempseed is another great source of protein. It contains 10 grams of protein per 28 grams. It is a good source of iron, magnesium, selenium, zinc, omega-3 and omega-6 fatty acids. It can be added to smoothies, salad dressings, morning muesli and protein bars.

Spelt and teff are from an ancient grain's category. Teff is gluten-free, whereas spelt contains gluten. They have 10–11 grams of protein per cooked cup. Spelt and teff are rich in iron, zinc, magnesium, selenium, manganese, phosphorus, fiber, B vitamins, and complex carbs. They can be used in a whole variety of dishes.

Spirulina is a blue-green alga and is rich in protein. 2 tablespoons will provide 8 grams of protein. It will also cover 22% of the daily iron and thiamin need and 42% of the daily need of copper. It is also a good source of, riboflavin, magnesium, manganese, essential fatty acids and potassium.

Green peas have 9 grams of protein per cooked cup in them. Green peas are good choice to get magnesium, iron, zinc, phosphorus, B vitamins and copper. 1 serving of green peas has enough in it to cover 1/4 of the daily need for vitamin A, C, K, fiber, manganese, folate and thiamine. Can be used in a whole variety of recipes.

Quinoa and amaranth are ancient or gluten-free grains. They provide 8–9 grams of protein per cooked cup and are complete sources of protein. Amaranth and quinoa are also a good source of iron, complex carbs, fiber, phosphorus, magnesium and manganese. Can be used in a whole variety of recipes.

Oats and oatmeal are standard in almost everyone's diet. ½ cup of dry oats provides 6 grams of protein and 4 grams of fiber. It is also a great source of zinc, folate, magnesium and phosphorus. Oats and oatmeal contain higher-quality protein than rice and wheat. Can be ground into flour, and used in a wide variety of recipes as flour and flakes.

Wild rice has more protein than other long-grain rice varieties, including brown rice and basmati. 1 cooked cup provides 7 grams of protein. It is also a good source of manganese, phosphorus fiber, copper, B vitamins and magnesium. Wild rice is not stripped of its bran and, thus, can contain arsenic in it. Therefore, washing wild rice before cooking is a must, and boiling it in a large amount of water should reduce the possible level of arsenic.

Chia seeds provide 6 grams of protein and 13 grams of fiber per 35 grams. They are also a good source of iron, selenium, calcium, magnesium, antioxidants and omega-3 fatty acids.

Nuts, seeds and products from them provide between 5–7 grams of protein per 28 grams. They are also a great source of iron, healthy fats, calcium, fiber, phosphorus, magnesium, vitamin E selenium, certain B vitamins and antioxidants.

Breakfast

Chocolate, Avocado, and Banana Smoothie

Preparation Time: 5 Minutes

Cooking Time: 0 Minutes

Servings: 1

Ingredients:

- One medium frozen banana
- Two small dates
- 1/2 cup steamed and chilled cauliflower florets

- 1/4 of a medium avocado
- One teaspoon cinnamon
- One tablespoon cacao powder
- 1/2 teaspoon sea salt
- One teaspoon maca
- 1/2 scoop of vanilla protein powder
- Two tablespoon cacao nibs
- One tablespoon almond fat
- 1 cup almond milk

Directions:

1. Put every ingredient in the instruction in a food processor or blender and then pulse for 2 to 3 MIN. At high speed until smooth.
2. Drench the smoothie into a glass and then serve.

Breakfast Sandwich

Preparation Time: 5 Minutes

Cooking Time: 6 Minutes

Servings: 4

Ingredients:

- ¼ of a medium avocado, sliced
- One vegan sausage patty
- Two teaspoon olive oil
- 1 cup kale
- 1/8 teaspoon salt
- 1/8 teaspoon black pepper

- 1 Tablespoon pepitas
- 1 English muffin, halved, toasted

For the Sauce:

- One teaspoon jalapeno, chopped
- 1/8 teaspoon smoky paprika
- One tablespoon mayonnaise, vegan

Directions:

1. Take a sauté pan, place it over medium heat, add oil and when hot, add the patty and cook for 2 MIN.
2. Then slip the patty, shove it to one side of the pan, add kale and pepitas to the other side, flavor with black pepper and salt, and cook for 2 to 3 MIN until kale has lessened.
3. When completed, remove the pan from heat and prepare the sauce by whisking its ingredients until combined.
4. Assemble the sandwich and spread mayonnaise on the inside of the muffin, leading with avocado slices and patty.
5. Before serving, top it with kale and pepitas.
6. Enjoy straight away

Potato Skillet Breakfast

Preparation Time: 5 Minutes

Cooking Time: 15 Minutes

Servings: 5

Ingredients:

- 1 ½ cup cooked black beans
- 1 1/4 pounds potatoes, diced
- 12 ounces spinach, destemmed
- 1 1/4 pounds red potatoes, diced

- Two small avocados, sliced, for topping
- One medium green bell pepper, diced
- One jalapeno, minced
- One large white onion, diced
- One medium red bell pepper, diced
- Three cloves of garlic, minced
- 1/2 teaspoon red chili powder
- 1/4 teaspoon salt
- One teaspoon cumin
- One tablespoon canola oil

Directions:

1. Turn on the oven, then set it to 400 degrees F and let it warm up.

2. In the meantime, take on a skillet pan. Over medium heat, add oil. Then, add potatoes, season with salt, chili powder, and cumin, stir until mixed and cook for 2 MIN.

3. Transfer pan into the oven and bake potatoes for 20 MIN until cooked, stirring midway.

4. Add the remaining onion, bell peppers, garlic, and jalapeno. For another 15 MIN. continue to roast it. Stirring midway, and remove the pan from heat.

5. Transfer pan over medium heat. Cook for 5 to 10 MIN. until potatoes are fully cooked.

6. Mix spinach and beans and cook for 3 MIN. Wait until the spinach leaves have wilted.

7. Top the skillet with cilantro and avocado and then serve.

Scrambled Tofu Breakfast Tacos

Preparation Time: 5 Minutes

Cooking Time: 10 Minutes

Servings: 4

Ingredients:

- 12 ounces tofu, pressed, drained
- 1/2 cup grape tomatoes, quartered

- One medium red pepper, diced
- One medium avocado, sliced
- One clove of garlic, minced
- 1/4 teaspoon ground turmeric
- 1/4 teaspoon ground black pepper
- 1/4 teaspoon salt
- 1/4 teaspoon cumin
- Eight corn tortillas
- One teaspoon olive oil

Directions:

1. Place a skillet over medium heat. Pour oil but wait until its hot, add pepper and garlic, and cook for 2 MIN.
2. Then add tofu and crumble it.
3. Sprinkle with black pepper, salt, and all the spices, stir and cook for 5 MIN.
4. Spread tofu between tortilla. Before serving, top with tomato and avocado.

Chickpea Flour Omelet

Preparation Time: 5 Minutes

Cooking Time: 12 Minutes

Servings: 1

Ingredients:

- 1/4 cup chickpea flour
- 1/2 teaspoon chopped chives
- ½ cup spinach, chopped
- 1/4 teaspoon turmeric

- 1/4 teaspoon garlic powder
- 1/8 teaspoon ground black pepper
- 1/2 teaspoon baking power
- One tablespoon nutritional yeast
- 1/2 teaspoon vegan egg
- 1/4 cup and one tablespoon water

Directions:

1. Take a bowl, place all the ingredients in it, except for spinach, whisk until combined, and let it stand for 5 MIN.
2. Then take a skillet pan, place it over low heat, grease it with oil and when hot, pour in prepared and cook for 3 MIN until edges are dry.
3. Then top half of the omelet with spinach, fold with the other half and continue cooking for 2 MIN.
4. Slide omelet to a plate and serve with ketchup.

Potato Carrot Salad

Preparation Time: 15 Minutes

Cooking Time: 10 Minutes

Servings: 6

Ingredients:

- Water
- Six potatoes, sliced into cubes
- Three carrots, sliced into cubes
- One tablespoon milk

- One tablespoon Dijon mustard
- ¼ cup mayonnaise
- Pepper to taste
- Two teaspoons fresh thyme, chopped
- One stalk celery, chopped
- Two scallions, chopped
- One slice turkey bacon, cooked crispy and crumbled

Directions:

1. Fill your pot with water.
2. Place it over medium-high heat.
3. Boil the potatoes and carrots for 10 to 15 minutes or until tender.
4. Drain and let cool.
5. In a bowl, mix the milk mustard, mayo, pepper, and thyme.
6. Stir in the potatoes, carrots, and celery.
7. Coat evenly with the sauce.
8. Cover and refrigerate for 4 hours.
9. Top with the scallions and turkey bacon bits before serving.

Mediterranean Salad

Preparation Time: 20 Minutes

Cooking Time: 5 Minutes

Servings: 2

Ingredients:

- Two teaspoons balsamic vinegar
- One tablespoon basil pesto
- 1 cup lettuce
- ¼ cup broccoli florets, chopped

- ½ cup zucchini, chopped
- ¼ cup tomato, chopped
- ¼ cup yellow bell pepper, chopped
- Two tablespoons feta cheese, crumbled

Directions:

1. Arrange the lettuce on a serving platter.
2. Top with the broccoli, zucchini, tomato, and bell pepper.
3. In a bowl, mix the vinegar and pesto.
4. Drizzle the dressing on top.
5. Sprinkle the feta cheese and serve.

High Protein Salad

Preparation Time: 5 Minutes

Cooking Time: 5 Minutes

Servings: 4

Ingredients:

Salad:

- One 15-oz can green kidney beans
- 2 4 tbsp capers
- 3 4 handfuls arugula
- 4 15-oz can lentils

Dressing:

- 1 tbsp caper brine
- 1 tbsp tamari
- 1 tbsp balsamic vinegar
- 2 tbsp peanut butter
- 2 tbsp hot sauce
- 1 tbsp tahini

Directions:

For the dressing:

1. In a bowl, stir together all the materials until they come together to form a smooth dressing.

For the salad:

2. Mix the beans, arugula, capers, and lentils. Top with the dressing and serve.

Vegan Wrap with Apples and Spicy Hummus

Preparation Time: 10 Minutes

Cooking Time: 0 Minutes

Servings: 2

Ingredients:

- One tortilla

- 6-7 tbsp Spicy Hummus (mix it with a few tbsp of salsa)
- Only some leaves of fresh spinach or romaine lettuce
- 1 tsp fresh lemon juice
- 1½ cups broccoli slaw
- ½ apple, sliced thin
- 4 tsp dairy-free plain unsweetened yogurt
- Salt and pepper

Directions:

3. Mix the yogurt and the lemon juice with the broccoli slaw. Add the salt and a dash of pepper for taste. Mix well and set aside.
4. Lay the tortilla flat.
5. Spread the spicy hummus over the tortilla.
6. Lay the lettuce down on the hummus.
7. On one half, pile the broccoli slaw on the lettuce.
8. Place the apple slices on the slaw.
9. Fold the sides of the tortilla up, starting with the end that has the apple and the slaw. Roll tightly.
10.   Cut it in half and serve.

Rice and Veggie Bowl

Preparation Time: 5 Minutes

Cooking Time: 15 Minutes

Servings: 6

Ingredients:

- 2 tbsp coconut oil
- 1 tsp ground cumin

- 1 tsp ground turmeric
- 1 tsp chili powder
- One red bell pepper, chopped
- 1 tsp tomato paste
- One bunch of broccolis, cut into bite-sized florets with short stems
- 1 tsp salt, to taste
- One large red onion, sliced
- Two garlic cloves, minced
- One head of cauliflower, sliced into bite-sized florets
- 2 cups cooked rice
- Newly ground black pepper to taste

Directions:

1. Heat the coconut grease over medium-high heat in a large pan
2. Wait until the oil is hot, stir in the turmeric, cumin, chili powder, salt, and tomato paste.
3. Cook the content for 1 minute. Stir repeatedly until the spices are fragrant.

4. Add the garlic and onion. Sauté for 3 minutes or until the onions are softened.
5. Add the broccoli, cauliflower, and bell pepper. Cover the pot. Cook for 3 to 4 minutes and stir occasionally.
6. Add the cooked rice. Stir so it will combine well with the vegetables—Cook for 2 to 3 minutes. Stir until the rice is warmed through.
7. Check the seasoning. And make adjustments to taste if desired.
8. Lower the heat and cook on low for 2 to 3 more minutes so the flavors will meld.
9. Serve with freshly ground black pepper.

Cucumber Tomato Chopped Salad

Preparation Time: 15 Minutes

Cooking Time: 0 Minutes

Servings: 6

Ingredients:

- ½ cup light mayonnaise
- One tablespoon lemon juice
- One tablespoon fresh dill, chopped
- One tablespoon chive, chopped
- ½ cup feta cheese, crumbled
- Salt and pepper to taste

- One red onion, chopped
- One cucumber, diced
- One radish, diced
- Three tomatoes, diced
- Chives, chopped

Directions:

1. Combine the mayo, lemon juice, fresh dill, chives, feta cheese, salt, and pepper in a bowl.
2. Mix well.
3. Stir in the onion, cucumber, radish, and tomatoes.
4. Coat evenly.
5. Garnish with the chopped chives.

Lunch

Instant Savory Gigante Beans

Preparation Time: 10-30 Minutes

Cooking Time: 55 Minutes

Servings: 6

Ingredients:

- 1 lb. Gigante Beans soaked overnight
- 1/2 cup olive oil
- One onion sliced
- Two cloves garlic crushed or minced
- One red bell pepper (cut into 1/3-inch pieces)
- Two carrots, sliced
- 1/2 tsp salt and ground black pepper
- Two tomatoes peeled, grated
- 1 Tbsp celery (chopped)
- 1 tbsp tomato paste (or ketchup)
- 3/4 tsp sweet paprika
- 1 tsp oregano

- 1 cup vegetable broth

Directions:

1. Soak Gigante beans overnight.
2. Press the SAUTÉ button on your Instant Pot and heat the oil.
3. Sauté onion, garlic, sweet pepper, carrots with a pinch of salt for 3 - 4 minutes; stir occasionally.
4. Add rinsed Gigante beans into your Instant Pot along with all remaining ingredients and stir well.
5. Latch lid into place and set on the MANUAL setting for 25 minutes.
6. When the beep sounds, quick release the pressure by pressing Cancel and twisting the steam handle to the Venting position.
7. Taste and adjust seasonings to taste.
8. Serve warm or cold.
9. Keep refrigerated.

Instant Turmeric Risotto

Preparation Time: 10-30 Minutes

Cooking Time: 40 Minutes

Servings: 4

Ingredients:

- 4 Tbsp olive oil
- 1 cup onion
- 1 tsp minced garlic
- 2 cups long-grain rice
- 3 cups vegetable broth
- 1/2 tsp paprika (smoked)
- 1/2 tsp turmeric
- 1/2 tsp nutmeg
- 2 Tbsp fresh basil leaves chopped
- Salt and ground black pepper to taste

Directions:

1. Press the SAUTÉ button on your Instant Pot and heat oil.

2. Sauté the onion and garlic with a pinch of salt until softened.

3. Add the rice and all leftover ingredients and stir well.

4. Lock the lid into place and set on and select the RICE button for 10 minutes.

5. Press Cancel when the timer beeps and carefully flip the Quick Release valve to let the pressure out.

6. Taste and adjust seasonings to taste.

7. Serve.

Nettle Soup with Rice

Preparation Time: 10-30 Minutes

Cooking Time: 40 Minutes

Servings: 5

Ingredients:

- 3 Tbsp of olive oil
- Two onions finely chopped
- Two cloves garlic finely chopped
- Salt and freshly ground black pepper
- Four medium potatoes cut into cubes
- 1 cup of rice
- 1 Tbsp arrowroot
- 2 cups vegetable broth
- 2 cups of water
- One bunch of young nettle leaves packed
- 1/2 cup fresh parsley finely chopped
- 1 tsp cumin

Directions:

1. Heat olive oil in a large pot.

2. Sauté onion and garlic with a pinch of salt until softened.

3. Add potato, rice, and arrowroot; sauté for 2 to 3 minutes.

4. Pour broth and water, stir well, cover and cook over medium heat for about 20 minutes.

5. Cook for about 30 to 45 minutes.

6. Add young nettle leaves, parsley, and cumin; stir and cook for 5 to 7 minutes.

7. Move the soup in a blender and blend until combined well.

8. Taste and adjust salt and pepper.

9. Serve hot.

Okra with Grated Tomatoes (Slow Cooker)

Preparation Time: 10-30 Minutes

Cooking Time: 3 Hours and 10 Minutes

Servings: 4

Ingredients:

- 2 lbs. fresh okra cleaned
- Two onions finely chopped
- Two cloves garlic finely sliced
- Two carrots sliced
- Two ripe tomatoes grated
- 1 cup of water
- 4 Tbsp olive oil
- Salt and ground black pepper
- 1 tbsp fresh parsley finely chopped

Directions:

1. Add okra in your Crock-Pot: sprinkle with a pinch of salt and pepper.

2. Add in chopped onion, garlic, carrots, and grated tomatoes; stir well.

3. Pour water and oil, season with the salt, pepper, and give a good stir.

4. Covering and cook on LOW for 2-4 hours or until tender.

5. Open the lid and add fresh parsley; stir.

6. Taste and adjust salt and pepper.

7. Serve hot.

Oven-Baked Smoked Lentil Burgers

Preparation Time: 10-30 Minutes

Cooking Time: 1 Hour and 20 Minutes

Servings: 6

Ingredients:

- 1 1/2 cups dried lentils
- 3 cups of water
- Salt and ground black pepper to taste
- 2 Tbsp olive oil
- One onion finely diced
- Two cloves minced garlic
- 1 cup button mushrooms sliced
- 2 Tbsp tomato paste
- 1/2 tsp fresh basil finely chopped
- 1 cup chopped almonds
- 3 tsp balsamic vinegar
- 3 Tbsp coconut amino
- 1 tsp liquid smoke
- 3/4 cup silken tofu soft

- 3/4 cup corn starch

Directions:

1. Cook lentils in salted water until tender or for about 30-35 minutes; rinse, drain, and set aside.
2. Heat oil in a frying skillet and sauté onion, garlic, and mushrooms for 4 to 5 minutes; stir occasionally.
3. Stir in the tomato paste, salt, basil, salt, and black pepper; cook for 2 to 3 minutes.
4. Stir in almonds, vinegar, coconut amino, liquid smoke, and lentils.
5. Remove from heat and stir in blended tofu and corn starch.
6. Keep stirring until all ingredients combined well.
7. Form mixture into patties and refrigerate for an hour.
8. Preheat oven to 350 F.
9. Line a baking dish with parchment paper and arrange patties on the pan.
10. Bake for 20 to 25 minutes.
11. Serve hot with buns, green salad, tomato sauce, etc.

Powerful Spinach and Mustard Leaves Puree

Preparation Time: 10-30 Minutes

Cooking Time: 50 Minutes

Servings: 4

Ingredients:

- 2 Tbsp almond butter
- One onion finely diced
- 2 Tbsp minced garlic
- 1 tsp salt and black pepper (or to taste)
- 1 lb. mustard leaves cleaned rinsed
- 1 lb. frozen spinach thawed
- 1 tsp coriander
- 1 tsp ground cumin
- 1/2 cup almond milk

Directions:

1. Press the SAUTÉ button on your Instant Pot and heat the almond butter.

2. Sauté onion, garlic, and a pinch of salt for 2-3 minutes; stir occasionally.

3. Add spinach and the mustard greens and stir for a minute or two.

4. Season with the salt and pepper, coriander, and cumin; give a good stir.

5. Lock lid into place and set on the MANUAL setting for 15 minutes.

6. Use Quick Release - turn the valve from sealing to venting to release the pressure.

7. Move mixture to a blender, add almond milk and blend until smooth.

8. Taste and adjust seasonings.

9. Serve.

Quinoa and Rice Stuffed Peppers (Oven-Baked)

Preparation Time: 10-30 Minutes

Cooking Time: 35 Minutes

Servings: 8

Ingredients:

- 3/4 cup long-grain rice
- Eight bell peppers (any color)
- 2 Tbsp olive oil
- One onion finely diced
- Two cloves chopped garlic
- One can (11 oz) crushed tomatoes
- 1 tsp cumin
- 1 tsp coriander
- 4 Tbsp ground walnuts
- 2 cups cooked quinoa
- 4 Tbsp chopped parsley
- Salt and ground black pepper to taste

Directions:

1. Preheat oven to 400 F/200 C.
2. Boil rice and drain in a colander.
3. Cut the top stem part of the pepper off, remove the remaining pith and seeds, rinse peppers.
4. Heat oil in a large frying skillet, and sauté onion and garlic until soft.
5. Add tomatoes, cumin, ground almonds, salt, pepper, and coriander; stir well and simmer for 2 minutes, stirring constantly.
6. Take away from the heat. Combine the rice, quinoa, and parsley; stir well.
7. Taste and adjust salt and pepper.
8. Fill the peppers with a mixture, and place peppers cut side-up in a baking dish, drizzle with little oil.
9. Bake for 15 minutes.
10. Serve warm.

Quinoa and Lentils with Crushed Tomato

Preparation Time: 10-30 Minutes

Cooking Time: 35 Minutes

Servings: 4

Ingredients:

- 4 Tbsp olive oil
- One medium onion, diced
- Two garlic cloves, minced
- Salt and ground black pepper to taste
- One can (15 oz) tomatoes crushed
- 1 cup vegetable broth
- 1/2 cup quinoa, washed and drained
- 1 cup cooked lentils
- 1 tsp chili powder
- 1 tsp cumin

Directions:

1. Heat oil in a pot and sauté the onion and garlic with the pinch of salt until soft.

2. Pour reserved tomatoes and vegetable broth, bring to boil, and stir well.

3. Stir in the quinoa, cover, and cook for 15 minutes; stir occasionally.

4. Add in lentils, chili powder, and cumin; cook for further 5 minutes.

5. Taste and adjust seasonings.

6. Serve immediately.

7. Keep refrigerated in a covered container for 4 - 5 days.

Silk Tofu Penne with Spinach

Preparation Time: 10-30 Minutes

Cooking Time: 25 Minutes

Servings: 4

Ingredients:

- 1 lb. penne, uncooked
- 12 oz of frozen spinach, thawed
- 1 cup silken tofu mashed
- 1/2 cup soy milk (unsweetened)
- 1/2 cup vegetable broth
- 1 Tbsp white wine vinegar
- 1/2 tsp Italian seasoning
- Salt and ground pepper to taste

Directions:

1. Cook penne pasta; rinse and drain in a colander.
2. Drain spinach well.
3. Place spinach with all remaining ingredients in a blender and beat until smooth.

4. Pour the spinach mixture over pasta.

5. Taste and adjust the salt and pepper.

6. Store pasta in a sealed container in the refrigerator for 3 to 5 days.

Slow-Cooked Butter Beans, Okra and Potatoes Stew

Preparation Time: 10-30 Minutes

Cooking Time: 6 Hours and 5 Minutes

Servings: 6

Ingredients:

- 2 cups frozen butter (lima) beans, thawed
- 1 cup frozen okra, thawed
- Two large russet potatoes cut into cubes
- One can (6 oz) whole-kernel corn, drained
- One large carrot sliced
- One green bell pepper finely chopped
- 1 cup green peas
- 1/2 cup chopped celery
- One medium onion finely chopped
- 2 cups vegetable broth
- Two cans (6 oz) tomato sauce
- 1 cup of water
- 1/2 tsp salt and newly ground black pepper

Directions:

1. Combine the real ingredients in your Slow Cooker; give a good stir.
2. Cover and cook on HIGH for 5 to 6 hours.
3. Taste adjusts seasonings and serve hot.

Dinner

Zucchini Omelet

Preparation Time: 10 Minutes

Cooking Time: 10 Minutes

Servings: 2

Ingredients:

- One teaspoon butter
- One zucchini, julienned
- Four eggs
- ¼ teaspoon fresh basil, chopped
- ¼ teaspoon red pepper flakes, crushed
- Salted and newly ground black pepper, to taste

Directions:

1. Preparing the Ingredients. Preheat the Instant Crisp Air Fryer to 355 degrees F.
2. Melt butter on a medium heat using a skillet.
3. Add zucchini and cook for about 3-4 minutes.

4. In a bowl, add the eggs, basil, red pepper flakes, salt, and black pepper and beat well.

5. Add cooked zucchini and gently stir to combine.

6. Air Frying. Transfer the mixture into the Instant Crisp Air Fryer pan. Lock the air fryer lid.

7. Cook for about 10 minutes. Also, you may opt to wait until it is done completely.

Zucchini Parmesan Chips

Preparation Time: 10 Minutes

Cooking Time: 8 Minutes

Servings: 10

Ingredients:

- ½ tsp. paprika
- ½ C. grated parmesan cheese
- ½ C. Italian breadcrumbs
- One lightly beaten egg
- Two thinly sliced zucchinis

Directions:

1. Preparing the Ingredients. Use a very sharp knife or mandolin slicer to slice zucchini as thinly as you can. Pat off extra moisture.
2. Beat egg with a pinch of pepper and salt and a bit of water.
3. Combine paprika, cheese, and breadcrumbs in a bowl.

4. Dip slices of zucchini into the egg mixture and then into breadcrumb mixture. Press gently to coat.

5. Air Frying. With olive oil cooking spray, mist coated zucchini slices. Place into your Instant Crisp Air Fryer in a single layer. Lock the air fryer lid. Set temperature to 350°F and set time to 8 minutes.

6. Sprinkle with salt and serve with salsa.

Cheesy Cauliflower Fritters

Preparation Time: 10 Minutes

Cooking Time: 7 Minutes

Servings: 8

Ingredients:

- ½ C. chopped parsley
- 1 C. Italian breadcrumbs
- 1/3 C. shredded mozzarella cheese
- 1/3 C. shredded sharp cheddar cheese
- One egg
- Two minced garlic cloves
- Three chopped scallions
- One head of cauliflower

Directions:

1. Preparing the Ingredients. Cut the cauliflower up into florets. Wash well and pat dry. Place into a food processor and pulse 20-30 seconds till it looks like rice.

2. Place the cauliflower rice in a bowl and mix with pepper, salt, egg, cheeses, breadcrumbs, garlic, and scallions.

3. With hands, form 15 patties of the mixture then add more breadcrumbs if needed.

4. Air Frying. With olive oil, spritz patties, and place into your Instant Crisp Air Fryer in a single layer. Lock the air fryer lid. Set temperature to 390°F, and set time to 7 minutes, flipping after 7 minutes.

Jalapeno Cheese Balls

Preparation Time: 10 Minutes

Cooking Time: 8 Minutes

Servings: 12

Ingredients:

- 4 ounces cream cheese
- 1/3 cup shredded mozzarella cheese
- 1/3 cup shredded Cheddar cheese
- Two jalapeños, finely chopped
- ½ cup breadcrumbs
- Two eggs
- ½ cup all-purpose flour
- Salt
- Pepper
- Cooking oil

Directions:

1. Preparing the Ingredients. Combine the cream cheese, mozzarella, Cheddar, and jalapeños in a medium bowl. Mix well.

2. Form the cheese mixture into balls about an inch thick. You may also use a small ice cream scoop. It works well.

3. Arrange the cheese balls on a sheet pan and place in the freezer for 15 minutes. It will help the cheese balls maintain their shape while frying.

4. Spray the Instant Crisp Air Fryer basket with cooking oil. Place the breadcrumbs in a small bowl. In another small bowl, beat the eggs. In the third small bowl, combine the flour with salt and pepper to taste, and mix well. Remove the cheese balls from the freezer. Plunge the cheese balls in the flour, then the eggs, and then the breadcrumbs.

5. Air Frying. Place the cheese balls in the Instant Crisp Air Fryer. Spray with cooking oil. Lock the air fryer lid— Cook for 8 minutes.

6. Open the Instant Crisp Air Fryer and flip the cheese balls. I recommend flipping them instead of shaking, so the

balls maintain their form. Cook an additional 4 minutes. Cool before serving.

Crispy Roasted Broccoli

Preparation Time: 10 Minutes

Cooking Time: 8 Minutes

Servings: 2

Ingredients:

- ¼ tsp. Masala
- ½ tsp. red chili powder
- ½ tsp. salt
- ¼ tsp. turmeric powder
- 1 tbsp. chickpea flour
- 2 tbsp. yogurt
- 1-pound broccoli

Directions:

1. Preparing the Ingredients. Cut broccoli up into florets. Immerse in a bowl of water with two teaspoons of salt for at least half an hour to remove impurities.
2. Take out broccoli florets from water and let drain. Wipe down thoroughly.

3. Mix all other ingredients to create a marinade.

4. Toss broccoli florets in the marinade. Cover and chill 15-30 minutes.

5. Air Frying. Preheat the Instant Crisp Air Fryer to 390 degrees. Place marinated broccoli florets into the fryer, lock the air fryer lid, set the temperature to 350°F, and set time to 10 minutes. Florets will be crispy when done.

Coconut Battered Cauliflower Bites

Preparation Time: 5 Minutes

Cooking Time: 20 Minutes

Servings: 4

Ingredients:

- salt and pepper to taste
- One flax egg or one tablespoon flaxseed meal + 3 tablespoon water
- One small cauliflower, cut into florets
- One teaspoon mixed spice
- ½ teaspoon mustard powder
- Two tablespoons maple syrup
- One clove of garlic, minced
- Two tablespoons soy sauce
- 1/3 cup oats flour
- 1/3 cup plain flour
- 1/3 cup desiccated coconut

Directions:

1. Preparing the Ingredients. In a mixing bowl, mix oats, flour, and desiccated coconut. Season with salt and pepper to taste. Set aside.

2. In another bowl, place the flax egg and add a pinch of salt to taste. Set aside.

3. Season the cauliflower with mixed spice and mustard powder.

4. Dredge the florets in the flax egg first, then in the flour mixture.

5. Air Frying. Place inside the Instant Crisp Air Fryer, lock the air fryer lid, and cook at 400°F or 15 minutes.

6. Meanwhile, place the maple syrup, garlic, and soy sauce in a saucepan and heat over medium flame. Wait for it to boil and adjust the heat to low until the sauce thickens.

7. After 15 minutes, take out the florets from the Instant Crisp Air Fryer and place them in the saucepan.

8. Toss to coat the florets and place inside the Instant Crisp Air Fryer and cook for another 5 minutes.

Crispy Jalapeno Coins

Preparation Time: 10 Minutes

Cooking Time: 5 Minutes

Servings: 2

Ingredients:

- One egg
- 2-3 tbsp. coconut flour
- One sliced and seeded jalapeno
- Pinch of garlic powder
- Pinch of onion powder
- Pinch of Cajun seasoning (optional)
- Pinch of pepper and salt

Directions:

1. Preparing the Ingredients. Ensure your Instant Crisp Air Fryer is preheated to 400 degrees.
2. Mix all dry ingredients.
3. Pat jalapeno slices dry. Dip coins into the egg wash and then into the dry mixture. Toss to coat thoroughly.

4. Add coated jalapeno slices to Instant Crisp Air Fryer in a singular layer. Spray with olive oil.

5. Air Frying. Lock the air fryer lid. Set temperature to 350°F and set time to 5 minutes. Cook just till crispy.

Buffalo Cauliflower

Preparation Time: 5 Minutes

Cooking Time: 15 Minutes

Servings: 2

Ingredients:

Cauliflower:

- 1 C. panko breadcrumbs
- 1 tsp. salt
- 4 C. cauliflower florets

Buffalo Coating:

- ¼ C. Vegan Buffalo sauce
- ¼ C. melted vegan butter

Directions:

1. Preparing the Ingredients. Melt butter in microwave and whisk in buffalo sauce.

2. Dip each cauliflower floret into buffalo mixture, ensuring it gets coated well. Holdover a bowl till floret is done dripping.

3. Mix breadcrumbs with salt.

4. Air Frying. Dredge dipped florets into breadcrumbs and place them into Instant Crisp Air Fryer. Lock the air fryer lid. Set temperature to 350°F and set time to 15 minutes. When slightly browned, they are ready to eat!

5. Serve with your favorite keto dipping sauce!

Grilled AHLT

Preparation Time: 5 Minutes

Cooking Time: 10 Minutes

Servings: 1

Ingredients:

- ¼ cup Classic Hummus
- Two slices whole-grain bread
- ¼ avocado, sliced
- ½ cup lettuce, chopped
- ½ tomato, sliced
- Pinch sea salt
- Pinch freshly ground black pepper
- One teaspoon olive oil, divided

Directions:

1. On each slice of bread, you need to spread some hummus. Then layer the avocado, lettuce, and tomato on one slice, sprinkle with salt and pepper, and top with the other slice.

2. Heat a skillet over medium heat, and drizzle ½ teaspoon of the olive oil just before putting the sandwich in the skillet. Cook for 3 to 5 minutes, then lift the sandwich with a spatula, drizzle the remaining ½ teaspoon olive oil into the skillet, and flip the sandwich to grill the other side for 3 5 minutes. Press it down with the spatula to seal the vegetables inside.

3. Once done, remove from the skillet and slice in half to serve.

Loaded Black Bean Pizza

Preparation Time: 10 Minutes

Cooking Time: 10 Minutes

Servings: 2

Ingredients:

- Two prebaked pizza crusts
- ½ cup Spicy Black Bean Dip
- One tomato, thinly sliced
- Pinch freshly ground black pepper
- One carrot, grated
- Pinch sea salt
- One red onion, thinly sliced
- One avocado, sliced

Directions:

1. Preheat the oven to 400°F.
2. Lay the two crusts out on a large baking sheet. Spread half the Spicy Black Bean Dip on each pizza crust. Then layer on the tomato slices with a pinch pepper if you like.

3. Sprinkle the grated carrot with the sea salt and lightly massage it in with your hands. Spread the carrot on top of the tomato, and then add the onion.

4. Pop the pizzas in the oven for 10 to 20 minutes, or until they are done to your taste.

5. Top the cooked pizzas with sliced avocado and another sprinkle of pepper.

Snacks

Strawberry Mango Shave Ice

Preparation Time: 5 Hours and 30 Minutes

Cooking Time: 0 Minutes

Servings: 3

Ingredients:

- ½ cup superfine sugar, divided
- 1½ cups mango juice
- One diced mango
- 32 oz diced strawberries
- ½ cup coconut, toasted

Directions:

1. Combine one cup of water and sugar to a pot over high heat and boil.
2. Remove from heat and add two more cups of water.
3. Freeze this mixture stirring once in 40 minutes.

4. Take a blender and add all remaining ingredients and blend until smooth.

5. Strain into a container with a pouring spout.

6. For serving, add ice into glasses and pour juice and mixture over them.

7. Serve and enjoy.

Cinnamon Apples

Preparation Time: 20 Minutes

Cooking Time: 1 Hour

Servings: 4

Ingredients:

- Two apples
- 1 tsp cinnamon

Directions:

1. Pre-heat stove to 220°F.
2. Core the apples or cut them into rounds with a sharp blade or mandolin slicer. Place the ingredients in a bowl and drizzle them with cinnamon. Use your hands to make sure the apples are coated completely.
3. Arrange the apple cuts in a single layer on a silicone tray or a baking sheet lined with parchment paper.
4. Bake for 1 hour then turn over the apples.
5. Bake for one more hour. Then, turn the oven off and leave the sheet in the stove until it cooled down.
6. Serve when needed or store in a sealed container for up to a week.

Roasted Chickpeas

Preparation Time: 10 Minutes

Cooking Time: 25 Minutes

Servings: 4

Ingredients:

- One can make chickpea, rinsed, drained
- 2 tsp freshly squeezed lemon juice
- 2 tsp tamari
- ½ tsp fresh rosemary, chopped
- 1/8 tsp sea salt
- 1/8 tsp pure maple syrup or agave nectar

Directions:

1. Preheat stove to 400°F. Line a baking sheet with parchment paper.
2. Toss all ingredients together and spread the chickpeas out on the baking sheet.
3. Roast for around 25 minutes, stirring the chickpeas every 5 minutes or so. Note, until the tamari and lemon

juice dry up, the chickpeas will seem delicate, not crunchy.

4. Serve hot or at room warmth for a snack.

Baked Sesame Fries

Preparation Time: 10 Minutes

Cooking Time: 20 Minutes

Servings: 4

Ingredients:

- 1 lb. Yukon potatoes, gold, cut into wedges, unpeeled
- 1 tbsp avocado, grapeseed
- 2 tbsp, seeds, sesame
- 1 tbsp potato starch
- 1 tbsp, yeast nutritional
- Generous pinch salt
- Black pepper

Directions:

1. Preheat stove to 425°F.
2. Delicately oil a baking sheet of metal or line it with parchment paper.
3. Toss potatoes with all the ingredients until covered; if seeds do not stick, drizzle a little more oil.

4. Scattered potatoes in an even layer onto the prepared sheet and bake for 20 to 25 minutes, tossing once halfway through, until the potatoes become crispy.

5. Serve with desired toppings.

No-Bake Coconut Chia Macaroons

Preparation Time: 2 Hours

Cooking Time: 0 Minutes

Servings: 6

Ingredients:

- 1 cup Shredded Coconut
- 2 tbsp Chia Seeds
- ½ cup Coconut Cream
- ½ cup Erythritol

Directions:

1. Combine all ingredients in a bowl. Mix until well combined.
2. Chill the mixture for about half or a quarter of an hour.
3. Once set, scoop the mixture into serving portions and roll into balls.
4. Return to the chiller for another hour.

Vegan Fudge Revel Bars

Preparation Time: 1 Hour

Cooking Time: Minutes

Servings: 12

Ingredients:

- 1 cup Almond Flour
- ¾ cup Erythritol
- ¾ cup Peanut Butter
- 1 tbsp Vanilla extract
- ½ cup Sugar-Free Chocolate Chips
- 2 tbsp Margarine

Directions:

1. Mix almond butter, coconut flour, erythritol, and vanilla extract in a bowl until well combined.
2. Press the mixture into a rectangular silicone mold and freeze for an hour to set.
3. Melt the chocolate chips with the margarine for 1-2 minutes in the microwave.

4. Pour melt down chocolate on top of the mold and chill for another hour to set.

5. Slice for serving.

Risotto Bites

Preparation Time: 15 Minutes

Cooking Time: 20 Minutes

Servings: 12

Ingredients:

- ½ cup panko breadcrumbs
- One teaspoon paprika
- One teaspoon chipotle powder or ground cayenne pepper
- *1 ½ cups cold* Green Pea Risotto
- Nonstick cooking spray

Directions:

1. Preheat the oven to 425ºF. Line a baking sheet with parchment paper.
2. On a large plate, combine the panko, paprika, and chipotle powder. Set aside.

3. Roll two tablespoons of the risotto into a ball. Gently roll in the breadcrumbs, and place on the prepared baking sheet. Repeat to make a total of 12 balls.

4. Spritz the tops of the risotto bites with nonstick cooking spray and bake for 15 to 20 minutes, until they begin to brown.

5. Cool totally before storing it in a large airtight container in a single layer (add a piece of parchment paper for a second layer) or a plastic freezer bag.

Taco Pita Pizzas

Preparation Time: 5 Minutes

Cooking Time: 7 Minutes

Servings: 4

Ingredients:

- Four sandwich-size pita bread pieces or Sandwich Thins
- 1 cup vegetarian refried beans
- 1 cup pizza sauce
- 1 cup chopped mushrooms
- One teaspoon minced jalapeño (optional)

Directions:

1. Preheat the oven to 400ºF.
2. Assemble four pizzas: On each pita, spread about ¼ cup of refried beans. Pour ¼ cup of pizza sauce over the beans and spread evenly. Add ¼ cup of mushrooms. Sprinkle ¼ teaspoon of minced jalapeño (if using) over the mushrooms.

3. Place the pizzas on the ready baking sheet and bake for 7 minutes.

4. Cool completely before placing each pizza in a freezer-safe plastic bag or store together in one large airtight, freezer-safe container with parchment paper between the pizzas.

Savory Seed Crackers

Preparation Time: 5 Minutes

Cooking Time: 50 Minutes

Servings: 20

Ingredients:

- ¾ cup pumpkin seeds (pepitas)
- ½ cup sunflower seeds
- ½ cup sesame seeds
- ¼ cup chia seeds
- One teaspoon minced garlic (about one clove)
- One teaspoon tamari or soy sauce
- One teaspoon vegan Worcestershire sauce
- ½ teaspoon ground cayenne pepper
- ½ teaspoon dried oregano
- ½ cup of water

Directions:

1. Preheat the oven to 325ºF. Line Up a rimmed baking sheet with parchment paper.

2. In a large bowl, combine the pumpkin seeds, sunflower seeds, sesame seeds, chia seeds, garlic, tamari, Worcestershire sauce, cayenne, oregano, and water. Move to the prepared baking sheet, spreading out to all sides.

3. Bake for 25 minutes. Remove the pan from the oven and flip the seed "dough" over so the wet side is up. Bake for an extra 20 to 25 minutes, until the sides are browned.

4. Cool completely before breaking up into 20 pieces. Divide evenly among four glass jars and close tightly with lids.

Stuffed Cherry Tomatoes

Preparation Time: 15 Minutes

Cooking Time: 0 Minutes

Servings: 6

Ingredients:

- 2 pints cherry tomatoes, tops removed, and centers scooped out
- Two avocados, mashed
- Juice of 1 lemon
- ½ red bell pepper, minced
- Four green onions (white and green parts), finely minced
- One tablespoon minced fresh tarragon
- Pinch of sea salt

Directions:

1. Place the cherry tomatoes open side up on a platter.
2. Combine avocado, lemon juice, bell pepper, scallions, tarragon, and salt.

3. Stir until well-combined. Scoop into the cherry tomatoes and serve immediately.

Desserts

Salted Caramel Chocolate Cups

Preparation Time: 5 Minutes

Cooking Time: 2 Minutes

Servings: 12

Ingredients:

- ¼ teaspoon sea salt granules
- 1 cup dark chocolate chips, unsweetened
- Two teaspoons coconut oil
- Six tablespoons caramel sauce

Directions:

1. Take a heatproof bowl, add chocolate chips and oil, stir until mixed, then microwave for 1 minute until melted, stir chocolate, and continue heating in the microwave for 30 seconds.

2. Take twelve mini muffin tins, line them with muffin liners, spoon a little bit of chocolate mixture into the

tins, spread the chocolate in the bottom and along the sides, and freeze for 10 minutes until set.

3. Then fill each cup with ½ tablespoon of caramel sauce, cover with remaining chocolate and freeze for another 2salt0 minutes until set.

4. When ready to eat, peel off liner from the cup, sprinkle with sauce, and serve.

Rainbow Fruit Salad

Preparation Time: 10 Minutes

Cooking Time: 0 Minutes

Servings: 4

Ingredients:

For the Fruit Salad:

- 1-pound strawberries, hulled, sliced
- 1 cup kiwis, halved, cubed
- 1 1/4 cups blueberries
- 1 1/3 cups blackberries
- 1 cup pineapple chunks

For the Maple Lime Dressing:

- Two teaspoons lime zest
- 1/4 cup maple syrup
- One tablespoon lime juice

Directions:

1. Prepare the salad, and for this, take a bowl, place all its ingredients, and toss until mixed.
2. Prepare the dressing, and for this, take a small bowl, place all its ingredients, and whisk well.
3. Drizzle the dressing over salad, toss until coated, and serve.

Coconut Oil Cookies

Preparation Time: 10 Minutes

Cooking Time: 10 Minutes

Servings: 15

Ingredients:

- 3 1/4 cup oats
- 1/2 teaspoons salt
- 2 cups coconut Sugar
- One teaspoon vanilla extract, unsweetened
- 1/4 cup cocoa powder
- 1/2 cup liquid Coconut Oil
- 1/2 cup peanut butter
- 1/2 cup cashew milk

Directions:

1. Use a saucepan, place it over medium heat, add all the ingredients except for oats and vanilla, stir until mixed, and then bring the mixture to boil.

2. Simmer the mixture for 4 minutes, mixing frequently, then remove the pan from heat and stir in vanilla.

3. Add oats stir until well mixed and then scoop the mixture on a plate lined with wax paper.

4. Serve straight away.

Chocolate Pudding

Preparation Time: 5 Minutes

Cooking Time: 0 Minutes

Servings: 4

Ingredients:

- 3/4 cup cocoa powder
- 12 ounces tofu, silken
- 1/3 cup almond milk, unsweetened
- 1/2 cup sugar
- Whipped cream for topping

Directions:

1. Place all the materials in a food processor and pulse for 2 minutes until smooth.
2. Distribute the pudding between four bowls, refrigerate for 15 minutes, then top with whipped topping and serve immediately.

Whipped Cream

Preparation Time: 5 Minutes

Cooking Time: 0 Minutes

Servings: 2

Ingredients:

- ¼ cup powdered sugar
- One teaspoon vanilla extract, unsweetened
- 14 ounces coconut milk, unsweetened, chilled

Directions:

1. Take a bowl, chill it overnight in the freezer, separate coconut milk and solid and add solid from coconut milk into the chilled bowl.
2. Add remaining ingredients and beat all of it for 3 minutes until smooth and well combined.
3. Serve straight away.

Peanut Butter Cheesecake

Preparation Time: 5 Minutes

Cooking Time: 15 Minutes

Servings: 8

Ingredients:

For the Crust:

- 1 cup dates, pitted, soaked in warm water for 10 minutes in water, drained
- 1/4 cup cocoa powder
- 3 Tablespoons melted coconut oil
- 1 cup rolled oats

For the Filling:

- One banana
- 1 1/2 cup cashews, soaked, drained
- 1/2 cup dates, pitted, soaked, drained
- 1/4 cup coconut oil
- One teaspoon vanilla extract, unsweetened
- 1/4 cup agave

- 1 cup peanut butter
- 1/2 cup coconut milk, chilled
- One tablespoon almond milk

For Garnish

- Two tablespoons chocolate chips
- Two tablespoons shredded coconut, unsweetened

Directions:

1. Prepare the crust, and for this, place all its ingredients in a food processor and pulse for 3 to 5 minutes until the thick paste comes together.
2. Take a pie pan, grease it with oil, pour crust mixture in it and spread and press the mixture evenly in the bottom part and along the sides, and freeze until required.
3. Prepare the filling and place all its ingredients in a food processor and pulse for 2 minutes until it is smooth.
4. Pour the filling into the prepared pan, smooth the top, sprinkle chocolate chips and coconut on top and freeze for 4 hours until set.
5. Cut cake into slices and then serve.

Matcha Coconut Cream Pie

Preparation Time: 5 Minutes

Cooking Time: 0 Minutes

Servings: 4

Ingredients:

For the Crust:

- 1/2 cup ground flaxseed
- 3/4 cup shredded dried coconut
- 1 cup Medjool dates, pitted
- 3/4 cup dehydrated buckwheat groats
- 1/4 teaspoons sea salt

For the Filling:

- 1 cup dried coconut flakes
- 4 cups of coconut meat
- 1/4 cup and 2 Tablespoons coconut nectar
- 1/2 Tablespoons vanilla extract, unsweetened
- 1/4 teaspoons sea salt
- 2/3 cup and 2 Tablespoons coconut butter

- One tablespoon matcha powder
- 1/2 cup coconut water

Directions:

1. Prepare the crust, and for this, place all its ingredients in a food processor and pulse for 3 to 5 minutes until the thick paste comes together.
2. Take a 6-inch springform pan, grease it with oil, place crust mixture in it and spread and press the mixture evenly in the bottom and along the sides, and freeze until required.
3. Prepare the filling and place all its ingredients in a food processor and pulse for 2 minutes until it is smooth.
4. In the prepared pan, pour the filling into the smooth the top, and freeze for 4 hours until set.
5. Cut pie into slices and then serve.

Brownie Batter

Preparation Time: 5 Minutes

Cooking Time: 0 Minutes

Servings: 4

Ingredients:

- 4 Medjool dates, pitted, soaked in warm water
- 1.5 ounces chocolate, unsweetened, melted
- Two tablespoons maple syrup
- Four tablespoons tahini
- ½ teaspoon vanilla extract, unsweetened
- One tablespoon cocoa powder, unsweetened
- 1/8 teaspoon sea salt
- 1/8 teaspoon espresso powder
- 2 to 4 tablespoons almond milk, unsweetened

Directions:

1. Combine all the ingredients use a food processor and process for 2 minutes until combined.
2. Set aside until required.

Strawberry Mousse

Preparation Time: 5 Minutes

Cooking Time: 15 Minutes

Servings: 4

Ingredients:

- 8 ounces coconut milk, unsweetened
- Two tablespoons honey
- Five strawberries

Directions:

1. Place berries in a blender and pulse until the smooth mixture comes together.
2. Place milk in a bowl, whisk until whipped, and then add remaining ingredients and stir until combined.
3. Refrigerate the mousse for 10 minutes and then serve.

Blueberry Mousse

Preparation Time: 20 Minutes

Cooking Time: 0 Minutes

Servings: 2

Ingredients:

- 1 cup wild blueberries
- 1 cup cashews, soaked for 10 minutes, drained
- 1/2 teaspoon berry powder
- Two tablespoons coconut oil, melted
- One tablespoon lemon juice
- One teaspoon vanilla extract, unsweetened
- 1/4 cup hot water

Directions:

1. Mix all the ingredients in a food processor and process for 2 minutes until smooth.
2. Set aside until required.

Conclusion

There are so many powerful and persuasive reasons to make a positive change and switch over to a plant-based diet. A plant-based diet will improve your quality of life, give you more energy and vitality, help you lose unwanted body fat, and it may even lengthen your years on this beautiful planet. As a bonus, by making the change you will be making a real and significant difference to our planet Earth's future. So much energy and fossil fuels are wasted by sourcing meat and other animal products, transporting them from place to place across miles and miles of road, and processing all of these animal products.

By switching to a plant-based diet, you will be greatly decreasing your carbon footprint and ensuring that fewer animals have to suffer at the hands of humans. And isn't that a good feeling?

Considering all the ethical reasons for switching to a plant-based diet, the enormous health benefits and improved quality of life are the icings on an already extremely appealing cake.

CPSIA information can be obtained
at www.ICGtesting.com
Printed in the USA
BVHW092248160521
607528BV00002B/294

9 781801 710398